Left of the Traffic Light

Devika Hardikar

BookLeaf Publishing

India | USA | UK

Presentation by *BookLeaf Publishing*

Web: www.bookleafpub.com

E-mail: info@bookleafpub.com

ISBN: 9789360948092

First edition 2024

DEDICATION

To the dreamers and the seekers,

those who wander left of the traffic light,

navigating life's uncharted paths

with courage and resilience,

this collection is for you.

May these poems serve as a guiding light

in moments of darkness,

a reminder that you are not alone,

and that beauty can be found

in the most unexpected places.

With love and admiration,

Devika Hardikar

ACKNOWLEDGEMENT

To the vibrant online forums that ignited the flame of my passion for writing, thank you for providing a platform where creativity knows no bounds. Your diverse community and endless inspiration have fueled my imagination and shaped my journey as a writer in ways I never imagined.

To my esteemed teachers and mentors, whose unwavering support and guidance have been a beacon of light on my path. Your belief in my potential and your willingness to invest time and energy in nurturing my talents have been invaluable. You have witnessed my growth, acknowledged my efforts, and encouraged me to pursue my passion with unwavering dedication.

To my beloved grandmother, whose innate talent for capturing ideas as they flow and bringing them to life on paper has been a source of inspiration and admiration. Your creative spirit and boundless imagination have been passed down to me, guiding my pen as I navigate the complexities of expression.

And to my dear parents, whose unconditional love and unwavering support have been the foundation upon which I have built my dreams. Thank you for nurturing my curiosity, for encouraging me to explore my passions, and for believing in me every step of the way. Your generosity, both in spirit and in action, has given me the world, and I am eternally grateful.

With deepest gratitude,

Devika Hardikar

PREFACE

Welcome to "Left of the Traffic Light," a poetic journey through the labyrinth of human emotion and experience. In this collection, you'll find a tapestry of verses woven from the threads of life's complexities—love and loss, societal struggles, and environmental crises. Each poem serves as a snapshot of a moment in time, capturing the essence of the human condition in all its beauty and turmoil.

As the author of this collection, I have drawn inspiration from the world around me—from the bustling streets of the city to the quiet solitude of nature's embrace. These poems are a reflection of my own experiences and observations, but they are also a reflection of the shared human experience—the universal truths and emotions that connect us all.

"Left of the Traffic Light" is divided into three distinct stages, each exploring a different aspect of life's journey. In the first stage, we confront the harsh realities of societal injustices and the pressing need for change. From poverty and inequality to discrimination and forgotten voices, these poems serve as a call to action, urging readers to confront the injustices that surround us.

In the second stage, we turn our gaze towards the looming specter of climate crisis. Through vivid imagery and evocative language, these poems paint a stark portrait of environmental devastation, reminding us of our collective responsibility to protect and preserve the planet for future generations.

Finally, in the third stage, we delve into the complexities of love and tragedy. From the innocent sparks of new romance to the heart-wrenching echoes of betrayal and loss, these poems explore the highs and lows of human relationships, offering a glimpse into the depths of the human soul.

It is my hope that "Left of the Traffic Light" will resonate with readers on a deep and personal level, sparking reflection, empathy, and perhaps even inspiration. May these poems serve as a reminder that, no matter how tumultuous life may seem, there is beauty to be found in every moment, and hope to be discovered in every turn of the road.

Thank you for joining me on this journey. Let us venture forth, together, left of the traffic light.

Warm regards,

Devika

Verge of Remarkable

We live on the edge
Of something remarkable

We stand upon the edge of time's great arc,
Where dreams converge and hopes embark.
In the space between what was and will be,
We sense the pulse of possibility.
We live on the verge of something rare,
Where the whispers of destiny fill the air.
In the realm of uncertainty, we take our stance,
Ready to seize the moment, to seize the chance.
A symphony of stars awaits our gaze,
As we navigate through life's intricate maze.
With each step forward, we dare to dream,
In the tapestry of life, we find our gleam.
We live on the verge of something grand,

With the power to shape our own land.
In the echo of history, we hear our call,
To rise, to strive, to break down the wall.
So let us embrace this moment profound,
Where the extraordinary waits to be found.
For in living on the verge, we embark,
On a journey towards something remarkable, a
spark.

Lackluster

The sky glows here.
Not every day,
Just everyday the planet cries,
A canvas painted with the hues of sorrow's
sighs.
In shades of amber and crimson, the tears are
shed,
As the earth mourns silently for the dreams long
dead.
Each dawn brings forth a new palette of despair,
A reflection of the burden that the land must
bear.
For every drop that falls, a story untold,
Of battles lost and futures sold.
The sky weeps for the forests razed to the
ground,
For the rivers choked with pollution profound.

It mourns the innocence lost to greed's cruel
hand,
And the scars etched upon the once pristine land.
Yet amidst the tears, there lies a glimmer of
hope,
A promise of redemption, a chance to cope.
For in the tears of the earth, there lies a plea,
To heal the wounds and set the planet free.
So let us heed the sky's lament, and strive,
To nurture the earth and keep its spirit alive.
For in the glow of every tear-stained sky,
Lies the hope for a future where all can fly.

Torrent

In the currents of life, we find ourselves adrift,
Caught in the leftward drift of circumstance,
Pulled by unseen forces, our course swift,
And swept away by fate's relentless dance.
Leftward we veer, away from the known,
Away from the safety of the familiar shore,
Into the depths where the wild winds are blown,
And the waves of uncertainty roar.
But amidst the chaos, a glimmer of light,
A chance to chart a course anew,
To turn from left and set things right,
And steer our ship towards skies of blue.
So let us grasp the helm and guide our way,
And navigate the leftward drift, come what may.

Lost in Left's Remorse

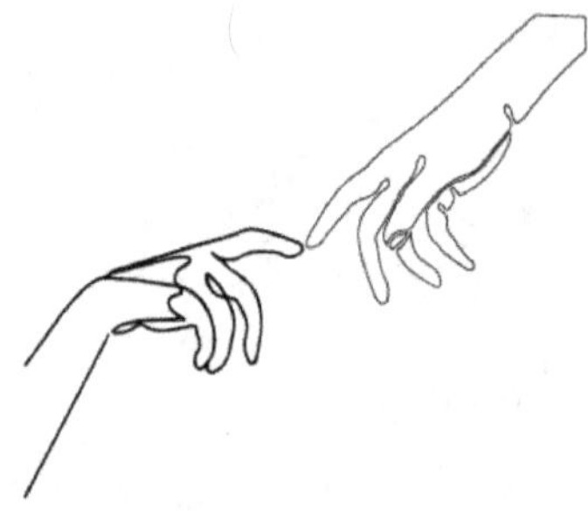

Upon the path where right should be, we stray,
Our footsteps falter, veering off course,
The signs ignored, the compass led astray,
And now we find ourselves in left's remorse.
The road less travelled, fraught with twists and
turns,
Each deviation leading us further from the light,
And though the destination our heart still yearns,
We wander lost in the shadows of the night.
But in the darkness, hope's ember still burns
bright,
A beacon calling us to find our way,
To turn from left and set our course aright,
And greet the dawn of a brand new day.
So let us heed the call and find our way back
home,
And leave behind the paths where left doth
roam.

A Neighbor's Lament

She lives in the room upstairs
She doesn't make a sound
Some think she never existed in the first place
She's always so quiet
But her presence
Everbearing
Some days she whispers
Others she roars
The day that I met her
I understood why she moved next door
She had a mission to complete

One day I heard her scream
so loud that my ears started to ring
The impact was sudden
My clothes began to become wet
My skin started to freeze

My lungs collapsed
My heart ached
My body began to sink

Some never knew she existed
Some never knew the burden
that came with having her as a neighbour
They never asked
They didn't notice her whispers
Didn't notice her banging on the walls

Some may never meet her
some might make her acquaintance
And others may end up with her as their
neighbour
They'll get to meet her
Someday.

Values We Held Dear

She was a virgin
a mystery to see.
In every age mark of purity,
Lying beneath obscurity
In whispers and glances, it's often derided,
a badge of honour, undecided.
But within its depths lies a power untold,
A choice, a defiance, a story to unfold.
she isn't just a label, you see,
But a declaration of autonomy, wild and free.
In a world that seeks to dictate our worth,
It's a reclaiming of self, a rebirth.
Society's gaze may cast doubts and shame,
Her calibre is to blame.
It's a canvas for self-discovery, unbound,
A journey of growth, profound.
So let us rewrite the narrative anew,

Embrace in all its hue.
For within its depths lies a revolution,
A celebration of self, a bold evolution.
Let society scoff, let them dissent,
It's more so a question of her content.
It's not a mark of weakness, but of strength,
A defiance of norms, a journey of immense.
So raise your banners, let your voices soar,
For her beauty, we shall adore.
In its complexity lies our liberation,
A symbol of defiance, of celebration.

Shadows of Urban Despair

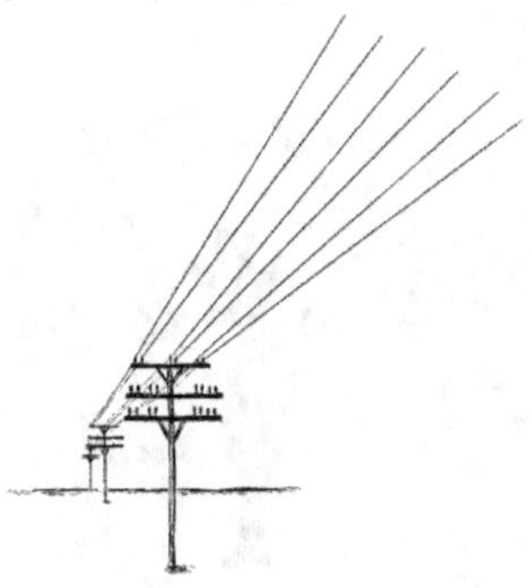

In shadows' dance, forgotten souls reside,
Where neon lights illuminate despair,
The pavement serves as bed, the cold, a bride,
Society's broken, silent, unaware.

Beneath the gleaming towers, hunger gnaws,
A symphony of sirens fills the night,
Where dreams decay and desperation crawls,
In alleyways where hope has taken flight.

Yet, in this urban maze, a heart may find,
Amidst the chaos, a whispered plea,
To heal the wounds of those left far behind,
And build a world where all can truly be.

Let empathy ignite the darkest skies,
And kindle flames where apathy belies.

We Have Yet to Panic

In the downturn's shadow, we march on,
Through trials deep, our spirit drawn.
Though storms may rage, and markets manic,
"We have yet to panic," our resolve, titanic.

Pulse, The City

Concrete veins stretch wide, a city's pulse,
Where dreams are crushed 'neath towering steel,
In hearts of stone, humanity's convulse.

The homeless drift, invisible, and false
Are promises of mercy, cold and real,
Concrete veins stretch wide, a city's pulse.

Beneath the glare, compassion's embers douse,
As shadows cloak the destitute's appeal,
In hearts of stone, humanity's convulse.

Society's divide, an ever-growing schism,
As riches flow, the poor are left to kneel,
Concrete veins stretch wide, a city's pulse.

In alleyways, the cries, the silent wails,
A testament to wounds that time won't heal,
In hearts of stone, humanity's convulse.

Yet in the midst of chaos, hope prevails,
A beacon for the lost, a chance to heal,
Concrete veins stretch wide, a city's pulse,
In hearts of stone, humanity's convulse.

Fading Stars, Fading Hope

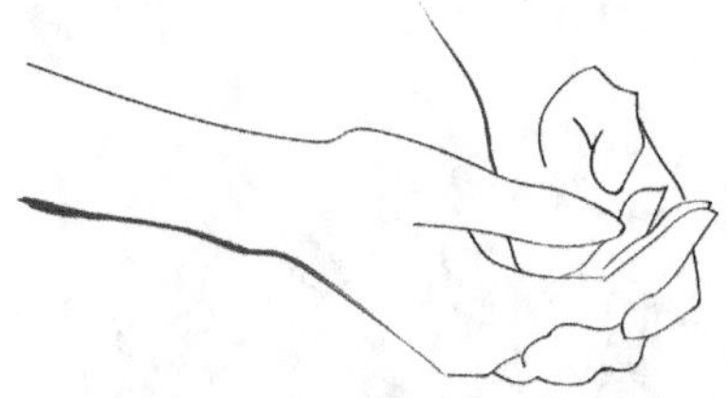

Once, in the velvet cloak of night,
The stars would dance in celestial array,
Yet now they fade, bereft of light.

Their brilliance dimmed, a solemn sight,
As city lights steal their display,
Once, in the velvet cloak of night.

Pollution's haze obscures their flight,
And clouds of ash obscure the way,
Yet now they fade, bereft of light.

A universe veiled, a cosmic blight,
In darkness now, they silently sway,
Once, in the velvet cloak of night.

Can we reclaim their shimmering might?
Or will they vanish without delay?
Yet now they fade, bereft of light,
Once, in the velvet cloak of night.

Melting Ice, Vanishing Legacy

In lands of eternal frost and snow,
Where glaciers reign and rivers flow,
A tale of tragedy unfolds,
As warming winds their fury holds.

Majestic ice, once firm and grand,
Now melts away, like grains of sand,
A legacy of ages past,
Vanishing fast, no time to last.

Polar bears roam, their kingdom lost,
Their icy realm, a tempest tossed,
As oceans rise, and shores recede,
A dire warning, we must heed.

For in this tale of ice and fire,
Lies the truth of our desire,
To tame the wild, at any cost,
Yet now we mourn what we have lost.

Beneath the Waves: A Cry for Help

Beneath the waves, a world of mystery,
Where creatures dwell in depths unknown,
Yet now they face an age of misery.

Coral bleached, and waters turned to stone,
Beneath the waves, a world of mystery,
Where creatures dwell in depths unknown.

Plastic islands drift, a grim debris,
A testament to actions we condone,
Beneath the waves, a world of mystery.

Can we reverse the damage that we've sown?
Or will the ocean's sorrow be our own?
Beneath the waves, a world of mystery,
Where creatures dwell in depths unknown.

Echoes of a Forest's Demise

Amidst the trees, a symphony of life,
A tapestry of green, a sanctuary,
Where ancient spirits whisper through the
leaves,
And shadows dance in nature's silent song.
Yet now the echoes fade, the trees stand still,
As greed consumes, forests start to fall.

The timber's call, a lure for those who fall,
The axe's bite, the harbinger of life,
As echoes of the past grow ever still,
A requiem for nature's lost sanctuary,
A mournful dirge, a tragic, silent song,
As chainsaws rend the silence of the leaves.

O, listen to the rustle of the leaves,
Their whispers carry warnings, hear the call,
To halt the march of progress, heed the song,
Before we lose the essence of all life,
Before we shatter nature's last sanctuary,

And silence reigns, the forest's voice now still.

Can we afford to let the forests still?
To let the wind's soft touch caress the leaves,
To keep intact this precious sanctuary,
Before the final tree begins to fall,
Before we choke the breath of all life,
And nature's song becomes a mournful song?

Let us rewrite the ending of this song,
Before the silence claims the forest's still,
Before we sever every thread of life,
Before the last leaf falls from barren leaves,
Before the final tree succumbs to fall,
And there's no trace of nature's sanctuary.

Preserve the sanctuary, the sacred song,
Before the silence falls, before the forests still,
Before the last leaf leaves, before the end of life.

Shadow's Bride

In whispered words, the silence lies,
As Shadow's bride, she softly sighs,
A chasm deep, a canyon wide,
Where love's demise does quietly reside.

Where hearts reside, in shadows hide,
Beneath her veil, they cower and bide,
The echoes fade, like tears we cried,
In her domain, where hope has died.

In empty rooms, where love has died,
She wanders through, a ghostly guide,
A silent scream, a soul defied,
As she claims those who dared to confide.

A love once fierce, now pacified,
By Shadow's bride, it is denied,
In memories, the pain implied,
Of hearts entwined, then cast aside.

Yet hope remains, though fate denied,
In the darkness, love still abides,
In fleeting moments, hearts collide,
With Shadow's bride, as shadows bide.

Through fractured bonds, we still confide,
In her embrace, where love resides,
In whispered words, the silence lies,
Where Shadow's bride, in darkness hides.

Shattered Fragments of Love

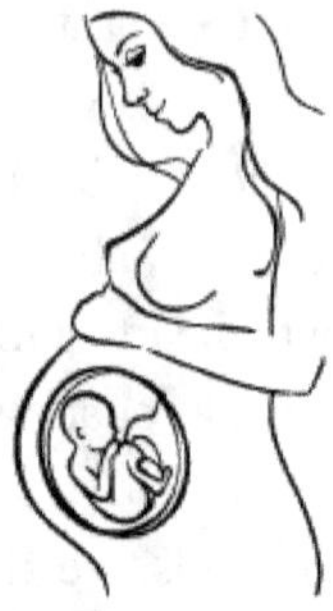

Love's fragments lie, torn,
Dreams unravel, hearts in thorns,
Echoes haunt the morn.

Will o Wisp

In the depths where shadows dance,
Willow the wisp casts its glance,
In the spaces where whispers fade,
Unspoken truths in darkness lay.

Through barren landscapes, it leads the way,
Guiding lost souls where memories stray,
But in its wake, only desolation's kiss,
As love's remnants vanish into the abyss.

Each empty room a solemn vow,
Echoing the ache, the loss we avow,
Once whole, now hollow, in its embrace,
As Willow's light illuminates the space.

Through corridors of memory, we roam,
Chasing dreams in the shadows' gloom,
But find only fleeting traces, a wisp's embrace,
As Willow's whispers fade without a trace.
Haunted by the specters of love's demise,
In the silence, Willow's light defies,
Until even ghosts surrender to its sway,
And into the void, they fade away.

Eros

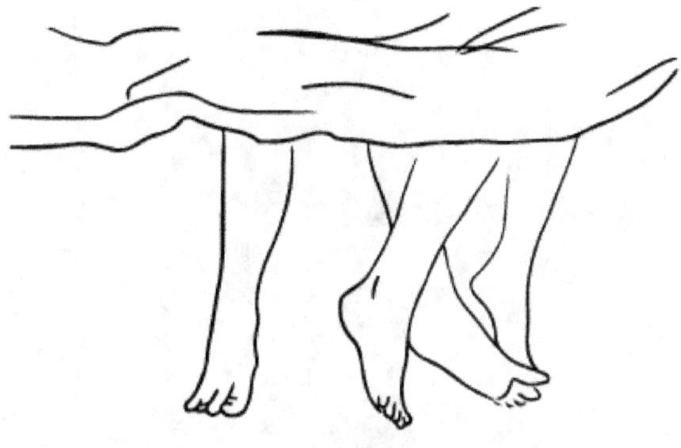

Love's arrow pierces deep,
In Eros' name, we fall,
Leaving wounds that never heal,
Aching for what once was whole.
In passion's grip, we find our fate,
Each step haunted by desire's call,
Echoes of a past, a lover's tale,
Where hearts entwined, but now we're small.
Haunted by the touch, the kiss,
Aching for what once we stole,
In Eros' game, we pay the price,
Leaving wounds that never heal, the toll.

Twilight of Our Love

In the twilight of our love,
We stood upon the precipice,
Our hearts entwined, our souls ablaze,
But now, the fire has died.
We were like two ships,
Lost in a tempestuous sea,
Tossed and turned by the waves of passion,
Until we were dashed upon the rocks.
Now, we wander through the wreckage,
Searching for fragments of what once was,
But find only echoes of our despair.
We were fools to think that love could conquer
all,
That we could defy the odds and find our
happily ever after,

But now, we are left with nothing but shattered
dreams.
And so we part ways,
Two souls adrift in a sea of regret,
And mourn the love that was lost to the winds of
time.

I Knew You Once

What am I to you?
Nobody.
Come close to me.
Stay away from me.
I saw you go.
I know.
I stayed behind.
I didn't see you.
I gather my strength to smile
I fought back tears
and you didn't see me.
and I walked away.
I didn't know what to do.
I had no choice.
But still, I'm not going to give up.
You should give up.

I want to show you my true self.
I can't let you do that.
This mask will one day fall
and you will know
You don't want to know
Who I am.
Who I am.

Rainbow

She was my canvas;
My palette of colour.

For blue, I drowned her
Until her face matched the sky.

For red, I dug blades under her skin
Until her blood ran in streams.

And for purple, I beat her
Until her flesh blossomed like lavender.

I saw how she flinched
How I plagued her little heart.

But shouldn't she be grateful?
I thought she liked art?

Dinner by 8, Dead by 9

In the hush of evening's descent,
Where shadows linger, time is spent,
A table set for two, bereft,
Of laughter's grace, love's sweet theft.

I knew heaven and hell would fight,
To have you on their side, that night.
Hell would send a child to persuade,
You join them, their plan unswayed.

But heaven, in its divine grace,
Would send death, to take its place.
A solemn visitor, at the door,
To claim your soul, forevermore.

As darkness falls and stars align,
A solitary tear, a silent sign,
For love once bloomed in this room so fine,
Now withered and lost, like a fleeting rhyme.

So here I sit, alone once more,
In this house of memories, forevermore,
Dinner by 8, dead by 9,
Love's final chapter, a bitter sign.

But in the quiet of this lonely hour,
Amidst the pain, amidst the dour,
I find solace in the silent night,
As I bid farewell to love's fading light.

For though love may falter, and hearts may
break,
In the stillness of night, I find my stake,
A glimmer of hope, a flickering flame,
In the darkness, I'll rise again.

And so I rise, from the ashes of despair,
With hope in my heart, and dreams to share,
For though love may die, it will rise anew,
In the hearts of the faithful, in me and you.

So let us raise our glasses high,
To love's sweet sorrow, to the tears we cry,
For though the night may be dark and long,

With each new dawn, we'll find our song.

And so I bid adieu to this house of sorrow,
To the memories lost, and the dreams of
tomorrow,
For, in the end, love will prevail,
In the hearts of the faithful, we will never fail.